VIRTUE STORIES

Oh that's Rude

Lalita Iyer

Om KIDZ
An imprint of Om Books International

When the snack break bell rang, the Year 2 children rushed out of the class. Snack or not, they never missed playing on the field. Especially since Ryan joined their class.

Ryan came up with the most interesting games to spend time: seven tiles, land and water, superpower games, catching cook, four corners, chain tag and much more.

Yes, Ryan had the best ideas but he was mostly angry or grumpy and never smiled easily. He had to be pleaded with to play with them. When someone didn't understand the rules of his game, he was quick to get angry and said some very rude things like "Oh, you are so dumb!" or something like that.

The last time, he told Megan, “I think you should just sit in a corner and watch. You are too slow for this game.” She was so upset, she burst into tears.

Yet, all the kids in the group wanted to be part of his cool games. They usually ignored his rudeness because playing with him was so much fun.

One day, Tomas from Spain joined their class. He was not very familiar with English, but he was very friendly and extremely polite. When he joined the group for their snack break game, he too was quite excited about playing the games that Ryan knew.

Now there were two problems; he did not understand the rules too well and he didn't know English too well. So he kept making mistakes, slowing down the game.

As usual, Ryan lost his temper and shouted at Tomas, "First learn English and then come and play with us!" Poor Tomas walked away with tears rolling down his cheeks. Luckily, he found another group of children to play board games with.

Now, the other eight children in Ryan's group really, really liked Tomas, and soon started missing him. Ryan was also beginning to get more and more annoying. They decided to spend snack time playing board games with Tomas. And guess what? Tomas could make his own board games! After a week, Ryan was left with nobody to play with. Everyone was now Team Tomas.

Ryan felt awfully lonely. He saw how his old group was having a great time with Tomas at the board games table.

That night he felt very upset with himself. He realised his rudeness had chased people out of his group. But what could he do now? Was it too late? There must be a way, he thought.

He finally had a plan.

Ryan walked into the school the next morning, and the first thing that he did was to find Tomas and the group of eight children. "Hi guys," he said, walking up to them. "I am really sorry. I have been so badly behaved these past few months. But it won't happen again. Promise."

The group looked at each other. No one spoke. They didn't know if Ryan actually meant what he was saying. And then Tomas spoke.

"It's okay. It happens. By the way, do you want to play Risk? I just learnt it. We could play at break time. "

After a couple of hours, when the snack break bell rang, you could see Ryan and Tomas and the entire gang discussing new game ideas and rules with an excited group on the field.

Ryan was never lonely, never rude and never without a smile ever again.